T0016909

Salvation Has Come

25 CHRISTMAS
DEVOTIONS IN LUKE

Salvation Has Come

GREGG MATTE

B&H
PUBLISHING
BRENTWOOD, TENNESSEE

Copyright © 2023 by Gregg Matte
All rights reserved.
Printed in the United States of America

978-1-4300-9193-6

Published by B&H Publishing Group
Brentwood, Tennessee

Dewey Decimal Classification: 242.33
Subject Heading: DEVOTIONAL LITERATURE / BIBLE. N.T.
LUKE—STUDY AND TEACHING / CHRISTMAS

Unless otherwise noted, all Scripture references are taken
from the Christian Standard Bible. Copyright © 2017
by Holman Bible Publishers. Used by permission. Christian
Standard Bible®, and CSB® are federally registered trademarks
of Holman Bible Publishers, all rights reserved.

Scripture references marked HCSB are taken from the Holman Christian
Standard Bible. Copyright © 1999, 2000, 2002, 2003, 2009 by
Holman Bible Publishers, Nashville Tennessee. All rights reserved.

Scripture references marked NIV are taken from the New
International Version®, NIV® copyright ©1973, 1978, 1984, 2011 by
Biblica, Inc.® Used by permission. All rights reserved worldwide.

Scripture references marked KJV are taken from
the King James Version, public domain.

Cover design by Jonathan Lewis, Jonlin Creative.
Photo by Andrey Danilovich/istock.
Author photo by Marlow Wise.

1 2 3 4 5 6 7 • 27 26 25 24 23

Dedication

I am Texan born and raised but spent Christmases growing up with family in Louisiana. To those who made Christmas special I dedicate this devotional guide.

To my Mom, Aunt Cheryl, Uncle Taylor, and my cousins Beth and Bryan—fun, fireworks, and running down the stairs on Brentwood Blvd. still makes me smile.

To my Dad, Uncle Dirk, my cousin Amanda, Granny and Pop (both now in heaven)—countless football games, Granny's gumbo, and LSU Tiger talk around the table, are great memories.

Thank you all for the wonderful Christmases growing up!

Acknowledgments

So grateful to my wife Kelly and our kids, Greyson and Valerie . . . affectionately known as Team Matte. Our advent devotionals around the Christmas tree through the years gave inspiration to this work. Our family is my biggest earthly blessing. Love you all!

I'm appreciative to my sister-in-law, Debbie Juern, whose Instagram post sparked the idea for this devotional. Thanks Debbie, Team Matte loves you and the Juern crew.

I'm thankful for my continued partnership with Lifeway, particularly Ben Mandrell, Mary Wiley, and Matt Hawkins. You guys make ideas into a reality!

The people and staff of Houston's First Baptist Church—our Christmas Eve candlelight services are one the highlights of my year. I'm grateful, humbled, and honored to be your shepherd. Don't tell anyone, but I think we have the best church on earth!

Contents

Introduction

Merry Christmas!

It's interesting where ideas can come from. While mindlessly scrolling Instagram one late November afternoon, I ran across my sister-in-law's post:

> New Christmas Tradition
> Beginning December 1
> read one chapter of
> the book of Luke in the Bible
> each day.
>
> There are 24 chapters.
> On Christmas Eve you will have read
> an entire account of Jesus's life
> and wake up Christmas morning
> knowing WHO and WHY
> we celebrate![1]

I thought, *What a great idea!*

Like using the thirty-one chapters of Proverbs for thirty-one days of the month, I set off in my December "quiet-time sled" with a chapter from the Gospel of Luke to match the date and write a devotional for each of Luke's twenty-four chapters and one more for Christmas day. The fruit of my daily reading of Luke now rests in your hands.

Our goal is to prepare our hearts for Christmas by delving into the life of Christ. My invitation to you is simple: read the chapter of Luke and the devotional entry that corresponds to the December date (chapter 1 on December 1, chapter 2 on December 2, and so on).

Over the next twenty-four days, we will read and reflect on the entire book of Luke. Then, on that most glorious of birthdays, December 25, we will know the *who* and the *why* of our Christmas worship.

As Chuck Swindoll wrote, "Luke had the mind of a scientist, the pen of a poet, and the heart of an artist. When you read his writing, it is as if you are there."[2]

With Luke's leadership, it is my hope we will celebrate on Christmas Day with a greater depth of understanding and joy! Let's go!

Your December guide,

Pastor Gregg

LUKE 1

The Lord Is with Us

We are beginning a wonderful twenty-five-day journey together today. It's not a marathon but a bit more than a sprint. Our goal is to push back the heightened stress or "bah humbug" of walking into another Christmas season and instead to prepare our hearts to truly celebrate His birth. The first chapter of Luke is a powerful platform for the Christmas story.

And the angel came to [Mary] and said, "Greetings, favored woman! The Lord is with you." Luke 1:28

The birth of Jesus was of such significance it required an *angelic* announcement. This baby announcement required far more than a social media post or card in the mail. The Messiah's birth meant *a word from heaven*: a star for the wise men, the heavenly hosts for the shepherds, and the angel Gabriel for Mary. Heaven declared to earth, in numerous ways, "The Son of God is coming to earth to save souls. And Mary, you are going to play a central part."

Obviously, to carry God's Son in your womb is a heavy calling. Could anything be more overwhelming when you are promised in marriage to another and in a culture where pregnancy out of wedlock could be punishable by death? Mary is deeply troubled and afraid. So the angel brings greetings and lets her know God is on this journey with her. She is favored by God, filled with grace, no fear needed. This Greek word for "favored" is used only one other time in the New Testament in Ephesians 1:6 "to the praise of His glorious grace that He favored us with in the Beloved" (HCSB). In a way, God is saying to Mary, "You are secure. I've got you." Ponder, yes, of course. Please ponder but don't panic. God is with you in the womb and in the world. God is going to lead the entire journey.

We soon see God will be with Mary and Joseph while riding the donkey, knocking on the door of the inn, in the stable, through the birth, in and out of Egypt, at the cross, and at the empty tomb.

Don't panic, but trust the Lord is with you, Mary.

Now none of us are going to carry such a responsibility this December, but we need the Lord's presence and guidance nonetheless. This month we will interact with family both distant and close, which is stress inducing on its own aside from the monthlong constant feeling of having too much to do with too little time to do it. As we speak, the calendar is filling with school, church, and personal activities, school is wrapping up the semester, and work is frantic. All these things and more are purposeful parts of lives, but they can be crushing if we believe we are walking through them alone. We need to know the Lord is with us. He is our power and strength. He is our guide and hope. He is the order in the chaos. The tasks are not too much for Him. He is with you.

Mary found God faithful and so will we in this season. Let's trust Him more deeply than the first eleven months of the year. His favor is upon His people through Jesus. Let's follow Luke through the plan of God—from the dark night of His birth to the empty tomb of His resurrection, realizing both were for us.

Merry Christmas!

Prayer: Lord, remind me and show me that You are with me. I want to walk with You as I anticipate and celebrate your birth! May Christmas come alive like never before in my heart.

LUKE 2

No Room in the Inn

Early in the season years ago, we brought all the Christmas decorations down from the attic—that annual tradition and necessary chore—to get ready for the blessed celebration of Christmas. Each box was full, but one of the most special to us was the one that contained our nativity scene, gifted to us by family many years ago.

I opened the box and carefully unpacked each character, placing them in their positions, but I couldn't find the baby Jesus. It's not much of a nativity with only Mary and Joseph and a few farm animals but no Savior of the world. The symbolism of the empty cradle struck me: without Jesus nothing else makes sense—both in the Christmas season and in life. He's the centerpiece of the nativity and the center point of our faith. You and I know this, but the innkeeper of Luke 2 was completely unaware of who he was turning away.

> *Then she gave birth to her firstborn son, and she*
> *wrapped him tightly in cloth and laid him in a manger,*
> *because there was no guest room available for them.*
> *Luke 2:7*

We don't read that the innkeeper was a terrible guy; we just read that his rooms were filled. He wasn't recorded for all eternity as slamming the door in Mary's face or telling Joseph to scram. He was just out of room and probably too busy to mess with a young couple while tending to a full inn.

The Feast of Tabernacles was happening so it was the inn's "busy season." In the midst of his equivalent to our presents to wrap, errands to run, and food in the oven, I imagine the innkeeper just motioning to the stable around back. Inns of this time period typically had a section for people and another for livestock. Since the human section was filled, the innkeeper resorted to saying, "You can be on the property just not in the heart of my home."

This is often where we end up in the season of Christmas—with fast-paced, busy calendars filled with endless to-do lists and too many credit card swipes to count. Jesus is on the property, somewhere, but not in the *center* of our Christmas.

The nativity is considered and likely on display, but a focus on the central member is missing. He's not central because we are already filled up. We've eaten too many chips before the enchiladas arrived. We've Cyber Monday-ed or Black Friday-ed so much the core of Christmas is misplaced, behind the house with the animals rather than in the center of it all.

There is no room in the inn of our hearts, even though much of what fills our time is *good*, like kids' activities, church presentations, parties to attend, travel plans to secure, and presents to buy. And that's true of me as a pastor, ironically, with Christmas messages to prepare. This flurry from Thanksgiving to Christmas leaves us filled to the brim but empty to the bone. There's just not enough room left in our hearts to ponder and praise.

Psalms 10:4 haunts: "In all his thoughts there is no room for God" (NIV).

But be encouraged! It's only December 2, and you can set out to have a Christmas season that looks different from years past. You can slow down, savoring the truth of what God has done through Jesus. You can prepare room for Him in your heart and life. It's fine to keep a busy schedule, but don't let the busy schedule keep you from the Hero of the nativity. A smile on our face and a word of praise on our lips creates room for the Savior in this season and any other.

Thankfully, with more searching in the box from the attic that stored our nativity, I found baby Jesus, and the manger was complete. He took His rightful place in the middle of the scene, the center of attention. May we rightly order our lives in the same way.

> Joy to the world, the Lord is come
> Let Earth receive her King
> **Let every heart prepare Him room.**[3]

Prayer: Jesus, I want You to dwell in the "inn" of my heart and life. Show me anything that is pushing You outside to the stable, and give me courage to do something about it so You can have Your rightful place in my life.

LUKE 3

Connected and Approved

The pleasure of God. What a thought that we are connected *and pleasing* to God!

It was first grade when my homework was returned by the teacher with an inscription at the top: "Good job!"

Not only that, but it was also accompanied by an orange scratch-and-sniff sticker saying something like, "Orange you smart!"

Approval, pleasure, and acknowledgment my little heart needed were there for all to see in bright red ink. Plus, there was the fragrant sticker! That *really* tipped it over the top!

In Luke 3 we see the approval of the highest sorts, well beyond cartoon fruit and man's praise. At Jesus's baptism God divides the heavens, descends the Holy Spirit like a dove, and says to His long-awaited Bethlehem-born Son:

> *"You are my beloved Son;*
> *with you I am well-pleased." Luke 3:22*

Words of connection and affirmation with a descending dove to boot. This heavenly statement is for us, too, this Christmas. As Christians, we are also God's children. Our objective is not to be the Savior of the world, but it is to connect with our heavenly Father.

As December begins, let your connection with God deepen. Warm blankets and hot chocolate by the fire make one yearn for quiet conversations. Thus, place a Bible in your lap and a prayer on your lips. The connection with God is wide open to us; He is splitting the heavens and descending like a dove to speak words of life to your soul.

The Holy Spirit lives inside every believer in Christ. His desire is to ensure we know the connection we have with God through Christ and . . .

Drum roll, please . . .

The Father *is*—present tense—well pleased with us. God thundered at the baptism of Jesus, "With you I am well-pleased" before His ministry had begun. Look at the next verse, "As he began his ministry, Jesus was about thirty years old."

Take this as your own: before Jesus ministered *for* God, He was pleasing *to* God. Meaning we are also pleasing to and loved by God before we have done a thing for Him. Whew! Heavenly approval is granted not gained.

Grace is throughout our salvation and our pleasure to God. We are connected and approved before any of our own accomplishments. In grace, our "homework" has a permanent inscription: "You're my child."

On the first Christmas morning in Bethlehem, we were on God's mind, in His heart, and a part of His plan. His great love for us stretched through time to find us before we had done a thing. As we follow His plan and walk in obedience, we discover this more and more. So today, let's place Jesus's baptism next to His birth and see the connection and approval of the Father in both. Allow this connection to inspire us to reflect on and live in the connection and approval of God in our lives.

At the top of our life's work will be penned in blood red, "Well done, my good and faithful servant." It might even have a divine scratch-and-sniff sticker saying, "You're berry loved!" Merry Christmas by His grace!

Prayer: Thank You, Lord, that in Christ I'm connected as Your child and pleasing to You. Let that be my focus as I live today.

LUKE 4

Different

Picture a hot summer day in Lafayette, Louisiana. I'm at my cousins' house, and we are begrudgingly helping with chores at the beckoning of my Aunt Cheryl. Being the only child that I am, I thought this would be a good place to insert some humor and secure a bit of personal attention. As would be the case, of course it backfired.

Somehow, we were on the subject of Christmas, though we were in the heat of a southern summer, and I chirped, "What's the big deal with Jesus's birthday? No one makes that big of a deal out of my birthday."

This was an attempt at humor not theology, but my aunt saw it as a teachable opportunity. Quickly, wisely, and clearly, she said, "Well Gregg, you're not the Savior of the world, are you?"

Touché.

She in one sentence identified something obvious: Jesus is different.

He's *other*. As the King of heaven, He's higher than the Christmas tree in Rockefeller Center. As the Healer of hearts, He's more beautiful than the garland on the mantle. As the path of salvation, He's sweeter than the pumpkin pie on Christmas Day. He is the Savior of the world!

He declares this as well,

> **The Spirit of the Lord is on me, because he has anointed me to preach good news to the poor. He has sent me to proclaim release to the captives and recovery of sight to the blind, to set free the oppressed, to proclaim the year of the Lord's favor. Luke 4:18–19**

These incredible verses were not just declared somewhere in the wilderness but in the Saturday synagogue of Nazareth, from the book of Isaiah, for the whole town to hear.

More than a carpenter's son, He is the Son of God. This difference was everything the people of Nazareth needed and everything we need as well. God's Spirit rested upon Him; it descended as a dove during His baptism. And He—God made flesh—was sent to bring good news to the poor, the captive, the oppressed, and the blind.

And we are the poor. Not just the poor in wealth but the poor in spirit. We are all bankrupt before God no matter what is in our checking account or how many zeros are to the right of the comma. Our poor hearts need salvation.

And we are the captive and the oppressed. His Words set us free, not from iron bars and chains but from habits, hang-ups, and addictions that keep us from Christ. Because He lived the perfect life and paid our ransom, Jesus has broken every bondage.

And we are the blind. In Christ we see God clearly, and we see the path He has designed. We are rich in Christ, we are free in

Christ, and we see in Christ, able to live for His glory. His favor rests upon us, and His heart is for us.

My aunt was right, I am definitely not the Savior of the world, and neither are you. The latest self-help routine, diet, gadget, political policy, or sleep aid can't change one thing about the truth of our spiritual situation. There is no true rescue from the things of this world, only further bondage. Yet the One who has set us free, Jesus, is different, higher, greater, closer, and by far, more powerful.

So take a page from my aunt's book and say it as a whisper from your heart toward all the things that will grab your attention today,

"Well, I'm not the Savior of the world, am I? I'm turning to Jesus who is."

Prayer: Jesus, You are the unrivaled Savior of the world. I gladly surrender. Do Your work in me today.

Incredible!

L uke 5 is an awe-inspiring chapter of incredible moments.

- After an all-nighter when they haven't had a bite, the disciples catch a miraculous load of fish at Jesus's direction.
- A leper is cleansed by just one touch from Jesus.
- A paralyzed man is lowered through the roof to the Lord's feet and healed.
- Matthew, a despised tax collector, is called to follow the sinless Christ and does.

All in a day's work for the Son of God but mind-blowing for "run of the mill" humans like us. The activities were so marvelous, halfway through the chapter Luke needed to insert a "hold on a minute" declaration to describe the scene:

> *Then everyone was astounded, and they were giving glory to God. And they were filled with awe and said, "We have seen incredible things today." Luke 5:26*

Be on the lookout for the incredible, the magnificent, and the miraculous this Christmas! God is always up to breathtaking works. At every turn, God is working in awe-inspiring ways, and this December will not disappoint.

We will see much of the tension present in our world in the first eleven months turn to calls for peace. Unity will sneak to the front row between opposing views. Stories of generosity will emerge from red kettles outside grocery stores and from toy drives, Christmas dinners for the homeless, gifts to one another and to the Lord's work through the church.

Amazingly gratitude, kindness, healing, and joy will move from back of mind to the tip of the tongue. Christmastime brings out the incredible.

The goal throughout the season is to be more than spectators of the incredible. Let's be participants. As Christians let's be champions of the kindness, love, care, truth, and gospel sharing—people in the formation of the incredible because we know the essence of Christmas awe.

The Savior of the world, prophesied through the ages, was born. The Son of God—filled with love, compassion, and justice—took up the cross to wash us clean, dwell in our hearts, and guide our lives. Incredible!

Even bigger and better than a net-breaking catch of fish, a dug-through roof, and miraculous healings, eternity Himself stepped into our world to provide the path to His world.

Look for the incredible today. One place I enjoy being reminded of the incredible during December is the rich lyrics of many Christmas songs. For example, see the incredible in the classic "O Holy Night,"

> *Verse 1:* Long lay the world in sin and error
>   pining,
> Till He appeared and the soul felt its worth.
>
> *Verse 3:* Truly He taught us to love one another;
> His law is love and His gospel is peace.
> Chains shall He break, for the slave is our
>   brother,
> And in His name all oppression shall cease.[4]

See the incredible and be the incredible in someone's life this December day!

Prayer: Lord, you are at work all around me. Focus my eyes on the incredible today so I can give You the praise you deserve.

Attitude of Heaven

There are numerous sayings regarding the power of our attitude. "Your attitude . . . determines your altitude."[5] "Attitude is everything."[6] "Have an attitude of gratitude."[7] And on goes the list.

But Jesus takes it past positive thinking to matters of the heart and soul. The beatitudes in Luke 6 (and more famously in Matthew 5) are more than slogans for a high school basketball team. They are traits and aspirations of the true believer. These one-liners are hard won wisdom and soul-infused guidance to the weariest of disciples.

> **Blessed are you who are poor,**
> **because the kingdom of God is yours. Luke 6:20**

What an irony to grasp while waiting in lines at cash registers and anticipating Amazon deliveries!

The woo of earthly wealth crescendos these busy buying weeks with food, Christmas clothes, décor, and a slew of gifts to buy. I'm not intending to be Scrooge here. Our family is doing the same things, but Jesus declares a contrarian path for the soul far beyond the wallet.

This path is poverty of the soul, a spiritual poverty aiming to possess heaven. We've seen Jesus highlight this before in Luke 4.

He is knocking again on the door for us to realize His wealth and our need.

Matthew 5:3 gives us a tad more to go on by saying the "poor in spirit." The acknowledged poverty of the heart will ultimately possess heaven. It is not an economic status but a heart declaration of our need for God. Our spirits, the core of our eternal existence is bankrupt until we call upon the Lord.

Beyond the exterior of the best self we put before the public is a chasm. Our sin separates us from God, but a Savior has come, sent by the grace of heaven and received by our faith on earth. This is Christmas! God sent His Son to our poverty to provide a path to heaven.

So the manger scene is a "run on the bank," if you will. Each character is poor in spirit and in need of a heavenly deposit.

The wise men journey in wonder of who would be worthy of a star to light the heavens. The shepherds leave flocks and fields to find the ultimate Shepherd. Mary and Joseph as parents are in awe of the heavenly Father's plan, and angels surround to gaze upon a greater sight than the gold of heaven: Immanuel come to earth in a feeding trough. The kingdom of heaven collides with the poverty of the world.

Our hearts, lives, and yes, even our attitudes are buffed into brilliance as we lay our spiritual poverty down as the only gift we have to offer before the One who holds heaven.

What a trade—our spiritual poverty for His heavenly riches!

Today, let's humbly but clearly admit we are spiritually poor without Christ. Maybe we're well dressed and entertained, but without God's indwelling we are empty. Yet admitting our poverty comes with an improbable blessing—the kingdom of heaven!

We are blessed with a relationship with Christ, guidance by the Holy Spirit, and an eternal home in heaven with the Father. Christmas trades our spiritual emptiness for complete fullness.

Second Corinthians 8:9 says it beautifully, "For you know the grace of our Lord Jesus Christ: Though he was rich, for your sake he became poor, so that by his poverty you might become rich."

Prayer: I am poor in spirit, and in the utmost humility, I ask You to make me rich with an attitude centered on the kingdom of God.

LUKE 7

Believe

She was at one cash register, and I was at another. My best description of her would be "a fun grandmother," the kind every kid wants to have. Her tennis shoes with a touch of glitter shone as she shifted to dig deep into her huge purse to find her wallet. The caring smile never left her face, but it was her Christmassy shirt with the one cursive word across the front that caused my heart to nod yes. The word was BELIEVE.

I'm not sure what exactly she was calling others to believe. It could have been Santa and the elves or the oh so ambiguous "spirit of Christmas," but my mind immediately went to my Savior born in Bethlehem. Yes! I do BELIEVE, and I want to BELIEVE more. I bet the same is true for you.

Our verse on this eighteenth day before Christmas captures it perfectly:

> *Jesus heard this and was amazed at him, and turning to the crowd following him, he said, "I tell you, I have not found so great a faith even in Israel." Luke 7:9*

This commendation that came as BELIEVE was the response of a Roman military man to Jesus's ability to heal his trusted servant, even at a distance. He knew Jesus didn't need to finish the journey to his house; He could just say the word and the healing would come. And come it did. This BELIEVER understood the authority of Christ. The centurion's belief trusted Jesus's power and the miraculous happened.

Life is tough, grief is real, and hospitals don't close in December. Yet we must still BELIEVE. As a pastor I'm honored to be a part of the hurts, heartaches, and the "hip hip hoorays" of people's lives. Regardless of which one is yours today, BELIEVE. Jesus came to planet Earth born of a virgin, for you and me, and He is powerful over it all.

He sent His Spirit who "helps us in our weakness" (Rom. 8:26). Weak and in need of help we most certainly are. This seventeen-letter Greek word for *help, synantilambanomai,* in Romans 8:26 is a really long word, but it is also rich with meaning!

First, it is in the present tense, meaning "an ongoing help." Second, it means "one who takes the other side, to help carry the load."[8]

Think of moving a heavy piece of furniture and someone lifts the other side as you walk together. Good news, God is on the other side lifting with you.

We all have heavy concerns to carry during the holidays, and no doubt, some are heavier than others. I can think of at least three families in our church whose situations bring tears to my eyes because of the weight they are carrying this Christmas.

I've encouraged them and I encourage you, BELIEVE.

Regardless of the odds you face or the hurts you feel, BELIEVE Jesus can bear the load and the Holy Spirit can take the heavy side. Throughout the Gospels we see Jesus at some of the most difficult moments we can face. Hunger, thirst, grief, storms, conflict—He is there as the bread of life, living water, resurrection and the life, water walker, and peacemaker. He is able to lift the heavy side.

The Spirit will help us carry the burdens we have laid at the Son's feet.

Belief is more than a cursive font on a cute holiday shirt. Belief is a depth of the soul brought forth in trial. The centurion believed so deeply that Jesus bragged on his faith to the crowd. He had strong belief in the right person amid sickness of a loved one, and it made all the difference.

I can't promise the healing will come in our time or on our terms, but I can tell you God is good.

Believing in Him is always the right call.

So wear it on your shirt for all the world to see, but most importantly, seal it in your heart as the foundation of life.

For the next eighteen days 'til Christmas and beyond, BELIEVE!

Prayer: Lord, increase my faith. I believe You can _____ .
Just say the word, Jesus, and it is done.

LUKE 8

Christmas Lights

The sun sets early these December days. Far from the long light of the summer, now I often journey home seeing headlights beginning to illuminate the road. But those are not the only lights turning on.

As I turn into my neighborhood, house after house is aglow: rooftops outlined in bulbs, trees wrapped to look like candy canes, Evergreens in the front windows twinkling. It's beginning to look a lot like Christmas, as the light overpowers the darkness of night!

We light the neighborhood to testify the Light of the world has come. Born into a dark world, on a dark night, God's light shone brightly in the manger. Where Jesus is, there is always the light of grace, kindness, wisdom, and hope.

When His birth was announced to the shepherds, the darkness disappeared and, "the glory of the Lord shone around them" (Luke 2:9). And remember the wise men were beckoned by a star lighting the path, "When they saw the star, they were overwhelmed with joy" (Matt. 2:10). Light is throughout the story of Jesus, and we celebrate the Light of the worlds entrance with lights on our houses and in and around our cities.

Since Jesus is the Light of lights, as Christians, we are personally to reflect His brightness. Like a thousand-watt bulb we go about our days, raise our kids, worship at church, and live our lives seeking to keep His light on display. Our "love, joy, peace, patience, kindness, goodness, faithfulness, gentleness, and self-control" shine as fruit of the Spirit to our dark world (Gal. 5:22–23).

As the houses in your neighborhood point to Christmas, we point to Christ.

> *"No one, after lighting a lamp, covers it with a basket or puts it under a bed, but puts it on a lampstand so that those who come in may see its light." Luke 8:16*

Our reflection of Christ is not a burden but a blessing. It is who we are, not just what we do. As our heart for God grows, so does our ability to reflect His light well.

Let me encourage you to fall deeper in love with Jesus as we near Christmas, and your light will burn brighter. We can and will shine the light to the overworked salesperson, distant neighbor, weary teacher. Let's be the brightest light in the room: a city set on a hill and a lamp on a lampstand because we are in love with the true Light of Bethlehem.

What a joy Christmas lights are!

Jump in the car with family and friends, and go for a drive to take them in. Let them symbolize Jesus as the light of the world and we as reflections of Him to a darkened world in need of a bright hope.

Prayer: Jesus, remind me with every Christmas light that You are the true and brightest light! Use me as well to shine Your light to those I meet today.

LUKE 9

Sacrifice

Sacrifice seems to be an out-of-place word at Christmas. Holiday, presents, gluttony, naps, and shopping . . .

But sacrifice is not usually the glitter font across the Christmas T-shirt of a "fun grandmother." Yet this sixteen-point Scrabble word is perfect for much of what we do in December. We sacrificially buy gifts for others, the kitchen bustles with cooking to feed those around the table, parents are up late reading assembly instructions, and then up before the sun watching bikes circling in the driveway. Sacrifice abounds at Christmas, but it is still not a theme word for the season.

Sacrifice could be defined as "an act of giving up something valued for the sake of something (someone) else regarded as more important."

Jesus defines sacrifice this way:

> *"If anyone wants to follow after me, let him deny himself, take up his cross daily, and follow me." Luke 9:23*

The call to follow Christ is a call to deny and crucify our desires and needs daily. We take our eyes off ourselves and place them on Christ, who then helps us shift our gaze to the needs of those around us.

Jesus is our primary love, others are second, and we are third (tertiary for the English majors among us).

Simply put, when in the right order—Jesus, Others, You—the result is always JOY.

Now there's a Christmas word, JOY! I can see that on a red and green Christmas sign at Hobby Lobby more easily than *sacrifice*. But the words are connected. Our Christmas season sacrifice brings Christmas season JOY.

Truly we don't see or feel the sacrifice because of the joy. The joy makes it better to give than to receive and to spend our time serving rather than consuming. The excitement of gifts and being served fades quickly, but sacrifice brings lasting joy.

So it is with following Christ. There is definite sacrifice, a daily cross we are to carry. Yet, on the other side of the price, is heavenly joy because His "yoke is easy" and His "burden is light" (Matt. 11:30) when your focus is on Jesus, Others, and then You.

The Latin root of our word *sacrifice* is *sacer*, which means "holy."[9] We get the words *sacred* and *sacrament* from this root as well. Thus, our sacrifice is a holy action unto God. Today, choose to sacrifice for Jesus and others as a "holy" decision and walk in joy. Take up your cross each day to follow Jesus, and He'll take care of the rest.

Prayer: God, bring death to selfishness and life to sacrifice today in my heart and steps. Reverently I put You and others first and trust You for the joy that follows.

LUKE 10

Mary of Bethany or Martha of Busyness?

The calendar says two weeks from today is Christmas Eve!

We respond conflicted, "How exciting. . . . Oh my, so much left to do. Yow! Two weeks, is that all? I need to cook . . . , buy . . . , attend . . . fix. . . ."

Somehow, in this final stretch of celebrating the Prince of peace, chaos so desperately wants to reign.

Take a deep breath and know two things. First, it will all get done, and if it doesn't, life will go on just fine. Second, losing our focus is losing our Christmas joy. The account of two sisters brings this perfectly into frame.

> **But Martha was distracted by her many tasks,**
> **and she came up and asked, "Lord, don't you care**
> **that my sister has left me to serve alone?**
> **So tell her to give me a hand." Luke 10:40**

Martha's not lacking in her hospitality, but she is *dis*tracted. This word in Greek means "to be drawn away." Traction toward the goal has been lost. Literally, *dis*traction ceases forward progress. The distractions have become central, while the Divine has become peripheral. The house needs to be cleaned and a meal prepared for Jesus. Therefore time can't be spent *with* Jesus.

Even though this took place in Bethany not Bethlehem, it highlights a common Christmas mistake. Good things draw us away from what is best. More than errands and tasks, are we spending time with Jesus? More than singing carols, are we worshipping with our lives? More than feeling the warmth of hot chocolate on a snowy evening, are we recognizing that God is the one who fills us through the work of the Holy Spirit who dwells inside the believer?

I'll tell on myself as a pastor: more than preparing Christmas messages, am I moved by the message of Christmas?

It is a temptation for all of us to scurry around and miss the point. Distractions abound, fighting for our time and attention and, most of all, our hearts. Yet the distracted is the one who pays the highest price. Here, Martha is too forceful in telling Jesus what to do and too snippy with her younger sister for my liking. As a result, written in the Scripture for generations to see, Jesus corrects Martha and encourages Mary's decision to sit at His feet, enjoying His presence. This moment is far better than checking the boxes on the to-do list. It has eternal consequences, while finishing tasks is temporal.

Believe me, I know things need to be done. They multiply, and without putting first things first, the tasks may get completed, but your heart will be far from Him. December is filled with tasks and engagements for all of us, but don't miss Jesus at Christmas. The world is great at removing Jesus from anything Christmas, but the people of God must be different. For us this isn't a celebration of winter weather, cozy feelings, or 50 percent off sales. It is *contemplation* of God sending His Son to earth, followed by the *celebration* of Jesus coming to have a relationship with me! Contemplation, not distraction, leads to true celebration of Christmas.

So yes, two weeks until December 24. Two weeks more of sitting at the feet of Jesus, choosing to walk in His peace instead of frantic action. Don't allow distraction to captivate your heart. Contemplate the Savior in the Gospel of Luke so you can celebrate Him rightly. Then you'll hold a candle at church and sing "Silent Night" surrounded by friends and family, astounded that the Savior has come.

Prayer: Jesus, I'm prone to distraction. Let me live these next two weeks with focus on You so I'll be ready to worship you wholeheartedly on Christmas morning.

LUKE 11

When the Doorbell Rings

What's your favorite Christmas movie: *It's a Wonderful Life, Elf, White Christmas, The Grinch* . . . ?

In a scene from the holiday classic *Christmas Vacation*, the doorbell rings as the extended family arrives for Christmas dinner. The sound at first is a typical doorbell pitch, but with each chime the sound gets lower until finally sounding like doomsday. Then the chaos of kin steps into the foyer, and pandemonium ensues.

As we near Christmas, do you have an increasing joy or dread as you think about when the doorbell rings in your near future?

> **"Every kingdom divided against itself is headed for destruction, and a house divided against itself falls."**
> **Luke 11:17**

Now, in this passage Jesus was talking about bigger issues than a relative getting on your last nerve, but it does illustrate the need for our homes and families to dwell in unity, even if it is only for twenty-four hours.

Christmas often puts us in settings outside our comfort zones and normal routines. Whether you are headed to the guest bedroom to slumber on a blow-up mattress or the one preparing the guest room for those who will crash there, the next two weeks will make all of us out of sorts to some degree. Meals and moments feel combustible, as you know all it takes for the fire to start is the hint of politics, a joke seasoned with a jab, or still being treated like a kid when you have your own kids.

Tensions or hidden frustrations are particularly apparent in today's world of divorce, which often makes Christmas vacation more like a Christmas tour to several houses. A married couple who both come from divorced homes might need to be at not one, two, three, but four places at once. Juggling time between each to try to be as fair as possible is tough. Four hours at house one and only three hours at house two because house three is waiting on your arrival before opening presents. This hectic people-pleasing can leave us feeling stretched beyond capacity.

This pace and peacekeeping effort can make the holidays feel like an annual dilemma where no one wins instead of a celebration. Let me offer four tips to keep us unified and not divided, at peace instead of blowing our top.

1. Pray your way in. Since you know the person, problem, or issues that will be a challenge, begin praying now. Prepare *your* heart through prayer.

2. Show others grace. Everyone is trying their best. Guilt trips and snide comments don't help. Support, encourage, be helpful, and give people the benefit of the doubt, even when you feel they don't deserve it. Recognize that moment when you may be tempted to react in an unhelpful manner or act selfishly. Remove yourself temporarily, if

necessary, and pray something like the prayer at the end of this day's devotional before you return.

3. Be grateful. These are your people. God has placed you here for a purpose and wants you to shine His light. Be thankful for where you have come from, what you can learn, and to whom you may reflect Jesus.

4. After the new year begins, evaluate what worked well and what didn't this year. Write it down in order to apply what you learned next Christmas. For example, this year's guest bedroom may need to become next year's hotel reservation. A little distance may help.

I hope you don't need any of this wisdom, but I bet you do. We all do.

Let God grow your spiritual maturity wherever your journey takes you over the next two weeks. Have fun, loosen up, and let God use you as a unifier. Even if "Aunt What's Her Name" declares she voted for "Candidate So-and-so" at the third house you've eaten at today, just smile and celebrate Jesus's birth.

Prayer: Lord, prepare my heart for the blessings and challenges of family. Let me be who You desire me to be. I'm grateful for my roots; they have helped make me who I am. I trust You to use me for Your glory whether I see it or not.

LUKE 12

Little Bitty Sheep

When the heavenly meets the earthly, something's got to give. In the Christmas account it is the knees of the person standing in front of the angel.

As our knees buckle, we are appropriately placed, bowing before the Lord. Reverent fear is something we should all carry. After all, we are talking about God, His dealings, and His plan. Reverent fear is first seen in Luke 1:13 when Zechariah encounters the angel Gabriel to prophesy the birth of John the Baptist.

Unfortunately, his fear became unbelief, and he could not speak for months. Then, just seventeen verses later in Luke 1:30, Mary meets Gabriel, and he offers the famous and familiar angelic phrase, "Do not be afraid." The Scripture goes on to say Mary ponders these things in her heart. Finally, the shepherds in Luke 2:10 receive the same "Don't be afraid" instruction as their knees buckled under their grass-stained tunics.

"Don't be afraid" statements are throughout the Christmas account because they are throughout the entire Bible. It's a frequent refrain for skittish and easily startled sheep like us, and it's a valid statement in a world where there is plenty to fear. Exterior evils and threats abound, so we lock the doors and stay in well-lit areas. While God is certainly present in our fear of physical realities, He often speaks even more deeply to the emotional and relational threats we face.

Matters of the heart are His favorite. Emotional pain hurts the worst. Not that I want either, but I would rather you break my arm than break my heart. Hit by a pitch and I'll walk to first base. Betray me and I will need a year of counseling. When you have a heartbreak, fear is a part of the scar tissue that protectively forms. We brace and barricade our tender places and even our spiritual places against future attack. Yet God remains tender and kind, shepherding us in our fear to trust Him.

> *"Don't be afraid, little flock, because your Father delights to give you the kingdom." Luke 12:32*

There's that heavenly phrase again for scared, earthly sheep: "Don't be afraid," spoken from the mouth of our good Shepherd. Eternally insightful, He refers to us with a double diminutive, "little flock." This is like saying small baby. Well, of course a baby is small, and, of course, the sheep are little. It is a doubling down to show Jesus's sweet endearment. We are timid and weak, but we are tremendously loved. The depths of God's love, shown so clearly in Bethlehem, puts us to rest. We can trust the Father with our physical lives, and the sheep trust their shepherd to protect them from wolves, but our Shepherd is worthy of an even deeper trust: trusting Him with our emotional and spiritual hearts. He is the Shepherd of our souls, and He is never intimidated by lions in the fields.

So I remind us of what we know and what we need to remember. When heaven and earth collide, our knees rightfully buckle in worshipful and reverent fear. Then that fear is transformed into faith by God's love. Therefore, don't be afraid of the exterior evils or the emotional hurts. Trust your Shepherd with your life and heart. In love, He delights to give us the kingdom of God. We little bitty sheep are deeply loved and blessed. Merry Christmas, little one.

Prayer: Shepherd, I'm aware of my fearfulness, yet I trust in Your strength! I'm grateful that I can find my courage in Your love.

The Little Things

Little things can make big changes. A dash of cinnamon or a touch of ginger flavors an entire meal, and a compliment said in passing can light up an entire day. Most women will tell you the small boxes hold the biggest gifts. More than jewelry or material possessions, the little things are a part of the kingdom of God.

> *"[The kingdom of God] is like a mustard seed
> that a man took and sowed in his garden. It grew
> and became a tree, and the birds of the sky
> nested in its branches." Luke 13:19*

Not much is smaller than a mustard seed, and nothing is bigger than the kingdom of God. Yet Jesus uses one to illustrate the other.

In a world of "bigger is better," we must stop and reframe the shot. The seeds we plant won't turn to harvest in an hour. True growth takes months and maybe even years. Mustard seeds are just one millimeter in length, the smallest of seeds in the ancient Near East, yet they grow into towering trees that provide rest for birds and shade for all. And yet, those who have faith the size of a tiny mustard seed can move mountains (Matt. 17:20).

Think about how God has used small things in your own life. A kind word from a friend, a lyric from a song, a word from a sermon, a hug from a loved one—the list could go on forever. Small things done in God's way can truly impact lives. Allow God to use you this Christmas to be faithful in the little things. Your faithfulness will add up to something big in God's math. We never know how He will use a mustard seed of faith.

In Jesus's math our seed of faith is like the kingdom of God. Amazing! We are touching heaven. His kingdom is eternal, worthy of praise, and earth changing. Bigger than anything we will ever be included in. Just think of the Lord's Prayer in Matthew 6, "For thine is the kingdom, the power and the glory, forever and ever. Amen" (v. 13 KJV). Small faith with big kingdom impact, and we are a part of it through the Christ of Christmas. Sign me up!

To illustrate God's use of little things, I'll make this the shortest devotional of our December journey together.

Go forth and do good in the little things, allow His power to be the big thing, and watch Him turn seeds into trees.

Prayer: Father, today will be filled with a million little things. Give me eyes to see and use the little things for Your glory.

LUKE 14

Take the Bad Seat

Jesus enjoys teaching with parables, and He loves to teach us humility. Luke 14 combines the two brilliantly.

We enter the scene at the house of a Pharisee, the religious leaders of Jesus's day. The Pharisees would choose the best seating for themselves, assuming they were the most important people in the room. Instead of allowing their religious training to move them to serve others in their community, they couldn't see past themselves.

Jesus knew they were looking for the most important seat. In Jewish culture, the most important seat was the center of the couch. In our culture, especially during football season, the most important seat is the recliner with the remote control, right? Regardless, if we are polite enough to let the seat go, our hearts can still struggle with an unspoken "me first" attitude. It's about the humble heart, not the prominent seat.

> *"For everyone who exalts himself will be humbled,*
> *and the one who humbles himself will be exalted."*
> *Luke 14:11*

Jesus desires humility. He told the people to take the worst seat, not the best. The last will be first and the first will be last (Matt. 20:16). Be assured, this is not about etiquette or seating arrangements for Jesus. It is about cultivating humility in our hearts, convictions, and practice. Pride is the root of all manner of sin. It never goes well, and God will always work to root it out of our lives. We will either be humble or be humbl*ed*! And I would much prefer to be humble *before* God than to be humbled *by* God.

Let's start low this Christmas. Let's be kind to the overworked salesperson. Let's show grace to family and friends. Let's bow at the lowly manger from a heart of gratitude. Let's humbly give gifts and humbly receive them as well.

Christmas provides an opportunity to break the "What's in it for me?" mindset. All of us have this mentality at times. "If I scratch your back, you will scratch mine. If I do this, you will do that. If I give you a $50 gift, I expect similar in return." We unknowingly seek reciprocity over heart-birthed humility, and Jesus wants to break that mindset in us. It is always about Jesus and others, especially as we near Christmas.

Jesus wants us to give and bless others without expecting anything in return. He wants Christmas humility that is illustrated in Christmas sacrifice. Here are a few action points:

- Buy a Christmas present for someone who isn't expecting it.
- Let someone go in front of you in line or have the parking spot.
- Ask if help is needed in the kitchen or with a task.

- Take the worst seat. Be humble instead of being humbled.

Let's actively choose humility to bless others and highlight Jesus this Christmas season.

Prayer: Lord, I humble myself before You. Let humility be sincerely from my heart and shown clearly in my life. I know true joy and purpose come from putting Jesus first, others second, and myself last.

LUKE 15

Party like an Octogenarian!

I wasn't late according to the invitation, but the street filled with Oldsmobiles, Buicks, and a handful of Cadillacs told me a different story. Night was just beginning to fall as I searched for a parking spot.

As their new thirty-something pastor, I was the guest of honor at the annual Christmas party for church members in their eighties, and I did not yet know the formal times listed didn't actually matter. They started early and ended early. They knew how to party and be in bed by 8:30! The food was great, the laughs were loud, and the fellowship was warm. It seems like an odd combination: senior adults—and Baptist ones at that—partying hard! I had so much fun that I attended seven or eight years in a row. I learned to arrive at this house first as I made my Christmas party rounds.

The reason they knew how to party is they knew *who* and *what* to celebrate. Long gone were the days of celebration revolving around music, popularity, or stiff drinks. This crew had been through a lot of life together: deaths, downturns, upswings, proud parenting, prodigal parenting, and a lot of Christmases. The latest fashion, coolest toy, or keeping up with the Joneses had no power over these grannies and gramps. As a result, they celebrated deep friendship, a strong church, and most importantly, the Savior born in a manger.

In this merrymaking of wise men and women, the important things were in view. They had prayed and seen the Savior at work for decades and would see Him face-to-face sooner rather than later. This reality informed their smiles as they kindly asked, "Would you like a piece of pie, Pastor?"

Luke 15 is also filled with important partying. The celebration gets louder and deeper with each discovery, producing celebration in heaven and on earth.

> *"I tell you, in the same way, there is joy in the presence*
> *of God's angels over one sinner who repents."*
> *Luke 15:10*

See, the heavenly party is driven by repentance. When we realize our sin and turn to our Savior, the eternal purposes of Bethlehem are realized. Jesus didn't come just to teach us or to become our life coach; He came to save us from the penalties of sin. He is the Savior of the world and desires to be the Savior of our souls—one heart at a time.

Luke 15 includes three parables: Ten coins and one was lost. One hundred sheep and the shepherd leaves the ninety-nine for the one that's lost. Then it gets personal, a lost son. A baby boy celebrated at birth, swaddled, rocked to sleep, fed thousands of meals at the dinner table, loved for years. And then he is lost, gone, running away from endless blessings by choice. A deeply loved part of the family and then a prodigal.

But in due time, far in the distance along the horizon is his silhouette. This lost child has repented and returned! Let's party! This is no coin or lamb but a person with a name, and he's been found!

As we attend Christmas parties, let's celebrate the right and righteous things. Past the clothes, desserts, and décor, a Savior is born. This birth is for us, so that we might see and know God; so that we might also repent and return to Him. In the chaos of the season, sometimes we lose sight of the gift Jesus is to us. We forget that He's made a way for us to be right with God because He died on the cross for our sin and was raised victorious. He calls us to repentance and return to the Father who loves us, and it is a heavenly party when we do!

My senior adult friends knew how to throw a Christmas party because they concentrated on the correct *who* and *what* of Christmas from the depths of their soul. Let's focus on the same and party—at least until 8:30 p.m. Ha!

Prayer: Father, give me the maturity to celebrate who and what really matters this Christmas.

LUKE 16

Go Tell It . . .

Sing it with me, "Go tell it on the mountain that Jesus Christ is born!"[10]

I remember singing this old Christmas hymn in elementary school in December. Believe it or not, I remember singing it in my *public* elementary school! My my, how times have changed. But those changes, and countless others, make it even more important to "tell it on the mountain."

The message of Jesus needs to be told from the highest of peaks to the lowest of valleys.

And what a message it is! God sent His Son out of love. So much love that He died on a cross and rose to life so we could have a relationship—a real, honest, and true relationship—with God through Jesus. This message changes our eternity but also our Monday mornings and mindsets, along with everything in between. It is the greatest message ever heard!

Luke tells a story in the sixteenth chapter about a rich man who had everything but salvation and a poor man, named Lazarus, who had nothing but salvation. Realizing eternity is longer than time on earth, the rich man pleads for his family to hear the message of salvation before it is too late.

> *"'Father [Abraham],' he said, 'then I beg you to send*
> *him to my father's house.'" Luke 16:27*

From the depths of his heart, while in the pain of eternal torment, he pleads: "Go tell it on the mountain. Go tell my family of this truth I now realize for their sake!" The rich man didn't care for others much while on earth, but separated from God, he understood what he was missing, and he didn't want anyone else to suffer his fate, especially his family.

This story reminds us that December is a time for sharing the message of Jesus. *Salvation* is what Christmas is about. *Salvation* is what we need personally and the message we must share. Salvation has come.

More than singing nostalgic songs about the weather, the trees, or the lights, let's sing about a Savior who has come! He has brought with Him the opportunity for our salvation. The greatest gift is not under the tree; He hung on the tree of the cross. His *presence*—not our *presents*—is *the* gift of Christmas.

With all of this in mind, how can you share the *real* meaning of Christmas with those around you? Here are a few ideas:

- Invite a friend to the Christmas Eve service or other Christmas events at church.
- Tell someone clearly why you are doing something kind. For example, "I'm doing _____ because Jesus saved my life."
- Say "Merry Christmas" as often as possible.
- Pray for someone. Be bold and pray for them in the moment, out loud, and sincerely rather

than telling them you'll be praying for them later (which means you'll likely forget).

- Look at your relationships and ask God to show you how He can use you.

What a Savior, what a joy, what a great time to "Go tell IT (the real story of Christmas) on the Mountain" or on your street! It's needed and worth it.

Prayer: Lord, use me for greater things. Give me an opportunity to tell someone of Your salvation.

LUKE 17

I Need More Faith

The apostles said to the Lord, "Increase our faith."
Luke 17:5

What a request! Amen!

Of all the presents we could receive, the increase of our faith is not only the best but also the longest lasting. Clothes will find a dark corner in the back of a drawer; toys will need new batteries; and electronics will be outdated in a few months. But a faith increase? That will help us from this December to the next and beyond. None of us know what the next calendar year holds, but we do know more faith will be required.

Where in your life do you need an increase of faith today? If you were to write down a place where you need increased faith, where would it be? Marriage, parenting, singleness, work, school, church, passion for God?

I've got good news. God can meet you even there. This verse is found immediately after a few warnings from Jesus in verses 1–4. Life is tough, and therefore we need an increase of faith to make it through.

How could this increase of faith come? The stirring up of faith is the work of the Spirit to generate trust in our Father's unfailing faithfulness, which is easy to say and so much more difficult to live. Yet "without faith it is impossible to please God" (Heb. 11:6), so faith is not a side item or an add-on to our relationship with God. Faith is central if we want to please God. By faith, the Old Testament saints believed the Messianic prophecies would come true. By faith the shepherds trusted the heavenly hosts who announced the arrival of the Savior in a manger; by faith the wise men followed the star; by faith the disciples followed Jesus; and today, by faith you and I join in His work on earth. All of those moments of faith are pleasing to God.

So, if faith is necessary to please God, we should investigate the places our faith is leaking or lacking. Where do we need shoring up? Is there a place you're a bit shaky? It could be trusting God with your finances, seeking to please others, fighting selfishness, and being self-absorbed. The list of possibilities is unending, but so is the *faith*fulness of God.

What's your faith challenge? Read a book, listen to a sermon or podcast on the subject, or ask a wise and trusted friend for advice to grow. More than that, ask God to increase your faith in that area. He is ready and willing. God can combine our head and heart so that we have a brilliantly consistent faith. Learn more by leaning closer.

So, if God is pleased by our faith, it should be a primary focus in our lives. This Advent season, these last eight days until Christmas, sprint to Jesus. He is the source and the subject of our faith. His resurrection can make our faith in God sure. He's kept His promise, and He will continue to. Seek Him and trust Him like never before.

With increased faith as our focus, life makes sense. As Matthew said, "Seek first the kingdom of God and his righteousness" (Matt. 6:33).

Increased faith in Jesus is the goal of Advent, this December devotional, and Christmas itself. Ask the Lord to increase your faith. Resist getting pulled into a worldly Christmas without Christ. Instead, ask for and receive the longest lasting and needed gift of heaven: increased faith!

Prayer: Lord, increase my faith. I especially need You to increase my faith with _____ in my life.

For the Kids

The wonder, the awe, the trust, the laughs, the fun, the joy . . .
It is often said Christmas is for the kids. This is both true
and false. True, if by kids we mean childlike faith. False, if by kids
we mean Christmas will ultimately be outgrown.

The birth of Jesus is for all of us, old and young. Let me make
a reach here, for sure Christmas is for every age, but the more
Christmases we have experienced, the more we need to become
like a child.

As I type, I've had more than fifty Christmases. All fun and
filled with calories. Yet I'm surprised how cynical life can make us—
has made me—at times. Having been around the block a few times,
we can often predict the next crack in the pavement that might trip
us or those we love. Hope gets eaten by reality, and reality darkens
by the day if we allow it. Too many calls about a friend diagnosed
with cancer, frequent news reports of chaos and harm, and the list
goes on. Instead of the widening eyes of childlike wonder, it's the
roll of the eyes in frustration. Life is hard and getting harder. I don't
laugh as much as I once did.

It isn't the six-year-old that needs to regain the wonder and awe
of Christmas; it's the fifty-six-year-old. We need a restoration of

childlike faith. We need to be children again, children of God. The Christian life is one of wonder and faith. Can I suggest a second childhood for those who have had a second birth?

> *Jesus, however, invited them: "Let the little children come to me, and don't stop them, because the kingdom of God belongs to such as these. Truly I tell you, whoever does not receive the kingdom of God like a little child will never enter it." Luke 18:16–17*

Trust in the Father is our goal. Our cynical and a bit jaded selves are called and directed to return to simple *trust*. We aren't beckoned to be child*ish* but child*like*. There's a difference. Childish is a place of immaturity and claims, "This is mine." Childlike in our faith is part of a journey, a continual journey, of maturing spiritually, and offers, "All is Yours."

This youthful, "all is Yours" Christmas wonder is highlighted in the Lord's Prayer. "Our Father . . . *Your will* be done on earth as it is in heaven" (Matt. 6:9–10). The "me" of life is shifted and reframed to the "He" of heaven. Whoa, me to He, what a change!

Childlike faith is not sugarplum fairies dancing in our heads; it is the Savior residing in our hearts. It is the maturity to trust the Father as a loved and precious child of His in the hardest of times. Sickness, mean people, deep pain, wondering and wandering while seeking what the next steps of life are—these are the times to be more childlike than ever before.

This Christmas let's all be children. Not childish but childlike. Let's fill our hearts, minds, and souls with great wonder because the Son, God's only child, was born in a manger. Let's sit amazed that shepherds in the fields interacted with angels. Let's be blown away, wide-eyed in awe that wise men bowed before a baby.

Let's see Christmas through the eyes of a child and grow in our faith. Fifty-plus Christmases in, I'm not naïve to life. I've been through tough times, but I'm not cynical either. I'm hopeful because I know the Father is with us and Jesus is alive!

Christmas *is* for the kids—kids like us.

Prayer: Father, please stir up a childlike joy with wonder of the blessings of Christmas in me.

LUKE 19

The Door Is Open

I'm sitting in a coffee shop a few blocks west of Times Square in Manhattan on a family trip to take in the NYC Christmas lights. I bet everyone knows I'm a tourist and not a local. My "Do *y'all* make lattes?" question sealed the deal. The door of this coffee shop is swinging open and closed over and over. The slamming has become a regular rhythm. The music continues with both tourists and the Monday morning regulars whose cadence quickens as they step outside the door into the December cold.

So it is with the Christmas story, opened and closed doors. Think back to December 2 when our devotion centered on the closed door of the innkeeper's house, closed because there was "no room in the inn." No room in the inn often becomes the truth about our hearts as well, stuffed full of "things" that don't actually fill us but leave no room for the only One who can.

Well, Luke 19 gives us a contrary account. Entering through the "coffee shop door," so to speak, is Zacchaeus. A wee little man with gold in his pockets from a career as a conniving and loathed tax collector. Even worse, Zacchaeus was the chief tax collector. As Jesus passes by, he climbs the trunk into the limbs to get and look. Before he could say "sycamore tree," Jesus is sitting in his house, and Zacchaeus is repenting of his sin. Note the contrast: the door to the innkeeper's house (someone literally in the hospitality business) was closed, while the door to the tax collector's house was wide open!

> *"Today salvation has come to this house," Jesus told him, "because he too is a son of Abraham. For the Son of Man has come to seek and save the lost."*
> Luke 19:9–10

I love this! The most despised man in town has flung open the door of his house and heart. Salvation came to his house, not just any house but *his* house.

Christmas came to Zacchaeus's house. There was room for Jesus in *this* inn, and it made all the difference.

We are in the single digits as we count down the days before the Christmas Eve candlelight service and the next glorious morning. Let's open the door, open our hearts, open our lives, and invite Jesus into our house. He is not only the Savior of the world. He is the Savior of the home of your heart! He comes near, and it only takes an open door to enjoy His presence.

As I finish typing day nineteen, the NYC coffee shop door twenty feet away has opened and closed countless times. People from all walks of life have entered the warm room for a warm cup. Opening the door is the first step in partaking of the menu. But let's take the illustration another step. Beyond opening the door to the Lord, let's take it off the hinges! Let's eliminate any hindrance, and say, "Come on in, Lord. I desire Christmas in my heart and home all year long."

Prayer: Please help the door of my heart to stay unlocked and wide open. Christmas through Christ, the joy of salvation. Come on in!

Eggs or Potatoes?

O ver the last nineteen days of this devotional, our trust in the Lord has grown. This month is not about the weather, the music, or wrapping paper but softened hearts preparing for the Baby who was born a King. As you read Luke 20, you experience the contrarian disposition of the religious leaders of Jesus's day, often questioning Him not out of curiosity but in hopes of setting a successful trap. As you read their question below, picture the stern and defensive faces asking in a harsh tone:

> *"Tell us, by what authority are you doing these things?*
> *Who is it who gave you this authority?" Luke 20:2*

You can sense the tension as they emphasize "these things." These things like healing, teaching, caring for the least of these, and helping those in need. "These things" they say as if they walked in on a disobedient toddler with a wagging finger.

We need more of "these things" in the world, like a million times more! Yet these leaders are blinded from the truth and are prideful. They have had enough of this Jesus's life-changing "things." Their goal is to put this rebel born in Bethlehem back in line, but they don't know who they are dealing with. He's not just an upstart religious entrepreneur. He is the Creator of the universe, and He has ultimate authority overall. Even them.

The heart of this confrontation is their questioning of His authority. As children would say, "Who made you the boss?" I wish this question was foreign to us and distant from our hearts, but unfortunately, the desire to be our own boss dwells deeply within us as well. Yet He is the boss, and He has the authority because all authority has been given to Him in heaven and on earth. He is the King and worthy of our worship.

God is big enough to manage our questions, and we see Jesus answer so many questions during His ministry. The problem here is the intent of the question. It's not really a question; it's *questioning*. There's a difference between a question and being questioned. There was a lack of trust in Jesus and a deep skepticism and disdain for Him by these leaders. A "Who do you think you are, mister?!" mindset.

Trusting the Lord is a crucial Christmas and Christian principle, even more so when we don't understand or agree with His instruction. Trust comes with a posture of humility in these moments rather than frustration or disdain because trust positions God as the rightful authority, the One who holds good and right plans for our lives and the world.

The characters of Christmas lived this out as examples to us. Zechariah didn't believe Gabriel's prophecy for John's birth, and he left the temple speechless for months as he learned to trust. Elizabeth, his wife, remained in seclusion for five months but believed God's favor was on her. Mary pondered it all in her heart and declared she was God's servant, willing to do as the angel said because she trusted God. Joseph needed a dream to set him straight, but when he awoke, he chose to walk faithfully, taking Mary as his wife and living under God's authority. Mary and Joseph lived lives of submission to Him, whether it was an Egyptian escape, a donkey ride to Bethlehem, or the burial of their completely innocent, thirty-three-year-old beloved Son.

Each one of these heroes in the nativity account trusted—instead of questioned—the authority of God. Pause to think this through: when their lives took a sharp turn, radically changing *their* plans and destiny, they didn't question God's authority. With prayerful and humble "Lord, increase my faith" moments (sans back talk or pushback), they processed and pondered, ultimately proceeding in obedience.

Whose authority will our hearts follow today? Is there an area of your life that is off limits to God? See, hot water makes an egg hard and a potato soft. Which will we be? I want to encourage us to soften our hearts this Christmas. Trust instead of question that God's authority is for our good. He has a plan that is different from the ones we come up with on our own, but celebrate because it is a good plan—the best and eternally sovereign plan for you.

Every month of our lives will offer hot-water opportunities to question God's authority, and December is no different. But don't harden like an egg, pushing back against God's good guidance. Instead, pray sincere "Lord, increase my faith" prayers. Live with a softened heart of trust even when you don't fully understand.

Prayer: Father, I know so little of what life will bring, and You know so much. Help me walk in faith trusting Your authority in my life.

A Hard Gift to Give

Less than one hundred hours until wrapping paper fills the floor and the presents are unveiled.

With this fact looming, stores are spending excessive amounts of marketing dollars to fill our eyes and inboxes with ads, and we are sprinting to the shopping finish line in the nick—St. Nick—of time. Celebrating the gift of Jesus with gifts for one another is a wonderful tradition and bonding experience for family and friends, and we are grateful to give and grateful to receive, but it is a lot to manage in the Christmas season

Yet the best gifts come from the depth of the heart and not the ad banner of a website. Luke 21 brings us to such a story.

He . . . saw a poor widow dropping in two tiny coins.
Luke 21:2

This woman is described by Jesus as poor, but not only poor, she is a widow. She lacked both money *and* marital love and support. Which hurts worse? Separation from financial security or loss of her husband? Well, of course the latter. Poverty is one thing; grief is another.

In biblical days the loss of a husband and loss of finances were synonymous. Therefore, *widow* is a frequent word in the Scripture alongside a call for care and concern. She is a person we give to—not take from—supported by the church or others because she would have few, if any, ways to provide for herself.

Let's focus on the widow of Luke 21:1–3. She is alone and possibly afraid. A woman who knows deep pain, has likely cried herself to sleep countless times, yet she courageously wakes up and walks through every day. Before the night her tears fall again. We assume this has been her response because we know the pain of our widowed friends. We've attended her husband's funeral and risen to our feet in respect as she walks into the worship center in grief, shock, and disbelief. We have shed our own tears for her and for him. The pain is real and palpable.

We've also seen the strength of these widows. Personally, as a pastor I'm amazed by these women, both old and young. Kindness and smiles grace their countenance as they greet me on Sunday. Strength and sincerity seem to be the fruit of processed grief. God has met them in their pain and faithfully made them a blessing to the rest of us. If you are a widow reading this, we honor you and love you. God is with you this Christmas and so are we.

The widow of Luke 21 is strong. In her poverty of heart and wallet she is an example to us. Her two coins amount to more than any others gave. Why? Because she gave from the depths, not from surplus. Her gift is sacrificial. She gave a gift she knew would be difficult to give. It would change the way she lived. She dug deep financially, but what is most notable is her faith. She deeply trusted God to care for her. She gave because she knew, from experience, God could be trusted. She walked through such pain, but we must believe that in it she saw the faithfulness of God as He provided for her over and over again. She knew He'd do it again.

A poor *widow* gave more than everyone else. God's math is different. It is not the amount of the gift but the willingness to sacrificially give, trusting Him all the way. He is interested in the heart.

She gave it all, and that is the call of Christ on the life of the Christian. Give it all—all our heart, all our pain, all our trust, all our worship, all our attention. The gifts of the heart—those that cost us—are the most meaningful, not just the ones wrapped in a box under a tree.

I'm sure you have a gift or two left to buy, but there are greater gifts we need to give. Give from the heart your listening ear, a kind word, a helping hand in the kitchen, a word of gratitude, or make a call to a widow you love.

Sacrificially give God your attention and worship this Christmas season. Give more of it than you feel you must give. It does us good to be stretched. The gifts God loves are from the heart. This Christmas lay your life down before the Savior as a gift.

Prayer: Lord, I pray for the widows in our church to feel the love of God deeply in these final December days. May I follow the example of the poor widow in Luke 21 and give my all from the depths of my heart.

LUKE 22

My, My, How Things Change

Life is wonderful and wild and weird. Boring and uneventful days seem to last forever, and yet life also can turn on a dime. Things change so quickly that before we know it we are in a totally different place. I wonder at times how I went from the Christmas morning kid running down the stairs in glee to the dad videoing my children doing the same. My, my, how things change.

Everyone says life goes by fast, but you don't really believe it until half your life has passed by.

As we enter Luke 22, things have changed for our Savior. The starry night of Luke 2 is thirty-three years in the rearview mirror. There are no longer shepherds and wise men bowing or a baby's tender skin being caressed by Mary. The days of the religious leaders quietly watching or asking questions are fleeting as the tone moves from questioning to murderous.

> **The men who were holding Jesus started mocking and beating him. Luke 22:63**

My, my, how things change. It is hard to read how these men treated the most loving and powerful person to walk the earth. Yet we know this is a part of the story of Christ. He was born, oh so sweetly born, to die a gruesome death.

The turn of events is excruciating. Baby Jesus is destined to be falsely accused, disrespectfully mocked, and gruesomely crucified. The cradle and the cross are distinctly connected for us. He was born and beaten to save our souls. What a tremendous love and commitment on our behalf!

We are nearing Christmas on the calendar, and the sweetness is growing. Yet in Luke 22 we see the cross looming on the horizon. This is good for us. The complete picture is necessary for our salvation *in* Christ and relationship *with* Christ. His birth and His burial are connected.

In the same regard, it is necessary for us to keep our joys and trials in the same windowpane. Life has ups and downs, twists and turns, but also long straightaways of peace. If we see joys and pains as disconnected, we will lose heart. Both are a part of normal life, and both are under God's love and command. He is with us and working in us on the highest summits and in the tearful valleys. God is painting a masterpiece in our lives with complementary dark and bright hues.

My, my, things can change—both from the cradle to the cross and in our lives from Christmas last year to Christmas this year. Trust God through the changes. Walk with God when the south wind blows. Look to the obedience of Jesus from the nativity of Luke 2 to the beatings of Luke 22. The fruit His life yielded is an example to the world and salvation for the believer's soul. Much has changed from December 22 last year to December 22 this year; that's how life goes. But we can still celebrate and trust God has a plan.

Prayer: Lord, give me the maturity and a long-horizon view to trust You through the changes of life.

LUKE 23

Trust from Kickoff to Final Whistle

College bowl games are as frequent these days as reruns of *It's a Wonderful Life.*

I enjoy this time of year watching a football game with the fireplace crackling. Regardless of the teams, it's a relaxing December blessing. One thing that is true for the upcoming National Championship game or a random no-name bowl is this: it is not how you start but how you finish. You can be up by twenty at halftime, but if you lose by two at the end of the fourth quarter, that first half lead means nothing. Similarly, life is not just about how you start or how you live the middle but how you finish.

Jesus's start was miraculous, born of a virgin, announced by angels, and all of this in the town of Bethlehem as prophesied in the Old Testament. He grew in wisdom and favor with God and man (Luke 2:52). His resume is filled with healings, miracles, kindness, and love. Now by Luke 23 things have changed from that first Christmas. There is no change in His character, but certainly everything has changed about His circumstances. The cradle has given way to the cross.

And Jesus called out with a loud voice, "Father, into your hands I entrust my spirit." Luke 23:46

His trust in the Father never wavered, even as He was tortured and died on a Roman cross. He was faithful from the start in the innkeeper's stable to the final moments on Calvary's hill. From a humble manger proclaimed by angels to a finish that proclaimed His eternal covenant, as the earth shook and the temple veil was torn, removing the separation between God and man.

As we have focused and feasted on the birth of Jesus this month, we have seen the key theme of trusting faith. The trust shown by the characters from the early chapters of Luke's Gospel is inspiring. Mary had to trust the words of Gabriel, Joseph had to trust his dream was from God, the shepherds trusted enough to begin to hike, and wise men believed enough to follow the star across great distances with gifts in tow.

Of course, Jesus trusted the most, leaving heavenly streets of gold for dusty, ancient paths. Now we see His faith to the end. He literally said, "It is finished." And through His faithfulness to the end, He completed the task and secured salvation for all who would trust Him.

Through His trust in the Father, He went to the cross and suffered mercilessly; and through our trust in Him, we don't have to do the same because He paid for sin once and for all. He didn't waver in His trust even once. Even with his dying breath, He entrusted His spirit to the Father. The Savior of the world entered as a baby and died on a cross, but that isn't where He stayed.

He trusted until the end, and we should too. Don't let your yuletide focus start well, only to buckle under seasonal stress before the appointed day.

Trust even more and let your faithfulness grow for the rest of the year, too. Let's be faithful until the end of the year and the end of our lives. From kickoff to final whistle, Jesus is worth trusting!

Prayer: God, I want to start well but, even more so, to finish well. Thank You for the example of faithfulness Jesus set for me from birth to death. Sustain me and show me what it means to finish well in this Christmas season.

LUKE 24

Be Amazed!

It seems a little odd to mention Easter on Christmas Eve, doesn't it? Shouldn't today's devotional discuss the starry night in Bethlehem, not an Easter sunrise?

Easter, in fact, is the perfect focus for Christmas Eve. The resurrection helps make sense of the marvelous birth. Christmas swaddling cloths filled with a Baby are now Easter linen cloths that wrapped a crucified Savior and yet were laid down by Him in an empty tomb. Easter is the confirmation of the divinity of Christ, the reason for celebration at Christmas.

> *Peter, however, got up and ran to the tomb. When he*
> *stooped to look in, he saw only the linen cloths.*
> *So he went away, amazed at what had happened.*
> Luke 24:12

The tomb is empty, and, to Peter's amazement, Jesus has risen!

We have the luxury of seeing the whole story of Jesus's life, death, and resurrection at once, able to see He was born for us and He rose for us. Jesus was the promised Messiah prophesied in the Old Testament, but those walking alongside Him often struggled to put the pieces together. The resurrection confirms what we know to be true as those who get to see the whole picture: Jesus lived a holy life, died by punitive crucifixion for our sins, and rose again, conquering death.

Now our salvation and our relationship with God through Christ are complete and accessible. Lots of babies have been born in Bethlehem, but only one has been resurrected in Jerusalem! Jesus is the Messiah, and He is alive today, seated at the right hand of the Father where He advocates for His people 24/7.

Take in the next forty-eight hours. Savor knowing God's full plan for redemption brought forth in Christ, and like Peter at the tomb, be amazed!

- Be amazed during your church's candlelight service tonight that Jesus is the light of the world!
- Be amazed by the blessing of family and friends. And even more profoundly that you are part of the family of God, and you are a friend of God.
- Be amazed by your favorite side dish at dinner because you have tasted and seen that the Lord is good (Ps. 34:8).
- Be amazed by gifts you will give and receive because they symbolize the gift of salvation in Christ (Eph. 2:8–9).
- Be amazed Christmas and Easter fit so perfectly together, transforming the world, beginning with you and me.
- Be amazed at a dark starry night birthed a glorious, sunrise Easter morning!

This Christmas we praise God for both the vulnerable cradle filled with the Son of God and His power to rise, leaving an empty tomb!

Prayer: Lord, Your plan is truly amazing! I'm grateful You sent Jesus for me. Thank You for Christmas, the cross, and Easter!

(By the way, congratulations on finishing the Gospel of Luke to prepare your heart for Christmas! I'm proud of you.)

Merry Christmas!

Like returning to the place you boarded an amazing amusement park ride, we are back to Luke 1, where we began. Our hair is blown back, and our smile can't be wiped off. Stories of wow and awe astound us, bringing both contemplation and joy. What a journey we've been on together, and we'll end at the beginning: the first Christmas Day.

Our path has taken us from December 1 to December 24, through the twenty-four chapters of the Gospel of Luke. Now we land at the day we have been looking forward to: Christmas Day! It is finally here. We've been waiting, shopping, hoping, praying for this day. Yippee, the calendar says December 25.

Gifts, food, fun, family, friends, and football await. What a day! No one is expecting return emails or attention toward solving pending problems. The office is closed and the schools are empty. So, what should we do with such a glorious, holy, and significant day?

Let's follow Mary's example step-by-step.

> *And Mary said: "My soul praises*
> *the greatness of the Lord." Luke 1:46*

- **My soul**—Mary speaks from the deepest and eternal part of her. The soul is the part of us that only God can cleanse and touch. From the depths of our soul come true praise and faith. This is the place we must start with God. He chose the color of our eyes and wants to use our hands, but deeper still He wants to own our souls. He wants us to live from our soul as well.

- **praises**—From depth of soul the highest worth is declared, and the deepest focus is given. How can we not praise Him? Look at all He has done in our lives. Praise is the strongest need of our heart and soul and most appropriate on Christmas Day.

- **the greatness**—Jesus is magnificent, incredible, high, and lifted up. What child is this who was born, lived, died, rose, saves, calls, heals, listens, cares, intercedes, and will return soon? It's God's only begotten Son. Jesus—the baby, the boy, the man, the crucified Savior—is the only reason for this season. Jesus is our great God, and today we celebrate that He came to earth for us.

- **of the Lord**—The good in my life and yours is not my doing, it's not your doing. It is not a gift of anyone on earth. Our lives are from Him and for Him. The breath in our lungs is "of the Lord." Therefore, it's all about the Lord every day. Especially today, Christmas Day. Give your life spiritually and practically to Him.

So today, on Christmas Day, let's eat too many side items and desserts, laugh until our face hurts, and enjoy the beautiful decorations and people we love. But don't miss it. Don't let the day go by without engaging your soul in praise of Jesus.

Learn from Mary, who was at the manger *and* the empty tomb. Praise God from the depths and sincerity of your soul for His greatness!

Thank you for taking this journey with me through the twenty-four chapters of Luke over the last twenty-five days of December.

A sincere, glorious Merry Christmas, from my family to yours.

Prayer: Lord, thank You for sending Jesus. Prophesied throughout the Old Testament and come to life in the New Testament. I'm grateful Jesus is the Savior of the world and also for little ole me. I'm forever grateful, especially on this Christmas Day, for Jesus's birth in Bethlehem and my new birth in Him!

Notes

1. On November 28, 2022, Gregg's sister-in-law, Debbie, reposted a meme from hearingwiththeheart.wordpress.com that has circulated social media for a few years, including on Instagram and Pinterest. That URL was not accessible March 14, 2023, when looking to assign appropriate credit. The text of that meme has been edited for grammar.

2. Charles R. Swindoll, "Introduction to Luke," *The Swindoll Study Bible* (Carol Stream, IL: Tyndale, 2017), 1275.

3. Isaac Watts, "Joy to the World," public domain.

4. Placide Cappeau, trans. John S. Dwight, "O Holy Night," public domain.

5. Zig Ziglar, accessed March 15, 2023, https://www.brainyquote.com/quotes/zig_ziglar_381975.

6. Jeff Keller, *Attitude Is Everything: Change Your Attitude . . . Change Your Life!* (Woodbury, NY: Attitude Is Everything, 2012).

7. Kaitlin Vogel, "Cultivating an 'Attitude of Gratitude' Can Vastly Improve Your Life—Here's How to Do It," Parade, February 11, 2023, parade.com/1223325/kaitlin-vogel/attitude-of-gratitude.

8. Logos Bible Software: *The Theological Dictionary of the New Testament*; Strong's Greek #4878.

9. "Sacrifice," *Britannica*, accessed March 15, 2023, https://www.britannica.com/topic/sacrifice-religion.

10. John W. Work, adapter, "Go Tell It on the Mountain," public domain.

Also available from
GREGG MATTE

Available wherever books are sold